Olive Miriam Johnson

1893-1979

Philip Wadner

2020

Published by Cade Books

©2020 Philip Wadner

All rights reserved.

ISBN 978-0-9931987-8-6

Philip Wadner has asserted his right under the Copyright, Designs and Patents Act 1988 to be identified as the author of this work.

This book is sold subject to the condition that it shall not, by way of trade or otherwise, be lent, resold, hired out, or otherwise circulated without the publisher's prior consent in any form of binding or cover other than that in which it is published and without a similar condition, including this condition, being imposed on the subsequent purchaser.

For Nanna,

who was always by my side.

Acknowledgements

This account would not have been possible without the extensive material available on the internet, and I express my gratitude to all those anonymous contributors who have made family history research possible in ways it has never been before. I am especially indebted to friend and author Dr. John Craddock for reading and commenting on my drafts, and to Colin Manning who brought to light some interesting aspects of the Jefferies family.

Contents

Acknowledgements iv
List of Photographs and Images vi
Preface vii
Overture ix
Background xiii
    Johnson xiv
    Robinson xv
Early Years (1893 - 1923) 1
    Olive Miriam Johnson 1
    Harry Edwin Jefferies 13
Great Yarmouth (1923-1936) 23
Bedford to Rugby (1936 - 1961) 33
Full Circle - Back to Bedford (1961-1979) 45
Epilogue 51

List of Photographs and Images

1 Foster Street, Bedford Then and Now 2
2 15 Battison Street 3
3 The Burnaby Arms 4
4 The Gordon Arms, Castle Road, Bedford 5
5 Soldiers from the Argyle and Sutherland Regiment at The Gordon Arms 1914 6
6 Behind The Gordon Arms 1915 7
7 9 Rosamond Road c1925, Robert and Jemima, Morris Bullnose Tourer 10
8 Olive Johnson c1922 11
9 Corporal Harry Edwin Jefferies, Royal Engineers c1920 18
10 Harry Edwin Jefferies WW1 Medals 19
11 Electric Light Works, Prebend Street, from across the River Ouse 20
12 Olive Johnson after her Engagement in 1923 Aged 29 23
13 Olive and Harry with Violet and Daisy (seated) at 9 Rosamond Road 24
14 Dorothy with Harry, his mother Charlotte, and his Grandparents 25
Edwin and Charlotte Brewer 25
15 Dorothy c1925 26
16 Olive and Dorothy Great Yarmouth c 1929 27
18 Great Yarmouth Power Transforming Station 29
19 Olive, Mother and Father, and Dorothy Great Yarmouth c1934 30
20 Jemima Jane Johnson c1920 33
22 Dorothy and John Wadner wedding 35
23 Robert Johnson c1920 37
25 2 Anderson Avenue, Rugby c1955 39
26 Hillman Minx 10HP 40
27 East Runton c1955 Olive with Dorothy, Philip and Patricia 41
28 Number 1 William Street, Rugby, Present Day 42
29 Olive visiting 2 Anderson Avenue, Rugby c1959 43
30 Olive and Walter (and Patricia behind bench) Caldecott Park c1959 44
31 Olive and Reginald Potter c1962 46
32 The Devonshire Arms, Dudley Street, Bedford 47
33 Philip, Olive and Patricia at Furzefield c1968 49

Preface

Had I written this book fifty years ago, it would have been far more revealing. Olive, my maternal grandmother and Nanna as she was known to the close family, was alive and could have answered many of my questions in the blink of an eye. My great uncles Archie and Bob could have helped fill in missing details, and my mother was there to tell me about her early life in Great Yarmouth.

Fifty years on, that golden window of opportunity to discover more about the person who probably influenced my life the most, has been missed. There is nobody left to ask.

It is not completely true that there 'is nobody left to ask', because so many genealogical records are available online, bringing history to life at the touch of a keyboard. However, it takes tenacity and lots of luck to find useful information. It also requires the ability to know when to stop looking, because often the answer to the question is simply not there.

Although when I started my research I had little knowledge of my maternal ancestry, a few facts had become vivid memories. They may have been vivid, but I soon discovered they were not all accurate. Of most help was a small and battered brown suitcase, probably a century old, containing a few documents and photographs accumulated after Olive's death in the late 1970s and the untimely passing of my mother in 1982.

Inside the suitcase, which had rested in our loft for longer than I can remember, were two old address books, a birthday book (these were fairly common through the first half of the twentieth century but lost their popularity to cheap throwaway diaries), and an autograph book dating back to the First World War. Also inside were various receipts, some photographs (including one of my great grandmother stuck onto wood so it would stand up by itself), wills and certificates of births, marriages and deaths. At the bottom of the case was a poignant document that entitled Olive a burial plot in Caister Cemetery alongside her first husband.

Not only does this book record the main episodes in Olive's life, and that of her close relatives, it also discloses many hitherto unknown facts. I am not going to describe them here, but will leave it to the reader to be as surprised as I was.

Philip Wadner

Overture

This short creative non-fiction work is adapted from the original, published in 'Three Courses', an anthology of writing by the author.

I was named Olive Miriam. Olive Miriam Johnson. Miriam after my father's older sister, who was born in 1870 but tragically only survived for nine months. The name Olive appears to have come out of the blue. My father, Robert Johnson, was born in Biddenham in 1866, and came from a long line of farm workers living in the countryside around the north-western corner of Bedford. Four years her senior, he married 19 year old Jemima Robinson from Houghton Conquest in 1889 after she fell pregnant with my brother Archie. The family lived in Foster Street, Bedford and that is where I was born towards the end of 1893.

My brother Bob arrived in 1897, and as the family grew we moved around the Bedford area and father tried his hand at different jobs. From farm labourer to railway carriage examiner to the W. H. Allen iron works. I was 13, when in 1906 mother had a baby boy, Stanley, who sadly died after 17 days. In 1907, we moved to Russell Street where father sold beer from an ale house. That was to be the start of a family history in the licensed trade. A year on, father took the license to The Burnaby Arms where we stayed until 1911 before moving to The Gordon Arms in Castle Road.

I had been singing since the age of 15, and taken lessons to train my voice. Although I appeared at events around the area, The Gordon Arms was large enough to give me the opportunity to entertain on home ground. It is from that point that my memories begin to become clearer. I remember walking through the bars early in the morning with the reek of stale beer, the stench of tobacco smoke and the earthy aroma of a well-trodden carpet playing tunes on my senses. It was as though the voices of the men from the night before were echoing off the brown-stained walls and hanging in the stagnant air.

Etched into my memories are the brave soldiers who passed through Bedford during The Great War, especially those of Scottish regiments who made a point of visiting The Gordon Arms. One iconic photograph was taken in 1914 when members of The Argyle and Sutherland Regiment gathered outside the pub. I was standing next to mother holding a Union Jack draped from a bedroom window, while father sat with the soldiers. A photographer captured the moment with a bright flash of magnesium powder, a puff of smoke hovering briefly above his head until blown away on the gentle summer breeze.

One evening when I had finished singing to a packed audience in the pub, I spotted a soldier writing inside a leather-bound autograph book which had rested on the bar since the beginning of the war. By the time I had pushed my way to the bar, the soldier had gone. The autograph book laid open at the page he had written upon:

"It is easy enough to be pleasant when life flows along with a song. But the man worthwhile is the man with a smile when everything goes horribly wrong."

I still have that autograph book. It reminds me that I found my 'man with a smile'. He lived just around the corner, and I knew him as little more than a passing acquaintance at first. We weren't walking out, but frequently exchanged pleasantries, and sometimes his deep brown eyes produced a suggestion in my mind which caught me by surprise. Harry Jefferies. But everyone called him Jeff.

It may have been some headiness remaining from the bar-room, or perhaps it was the scent of that summer evening when Jeff walked me home from the pub, or the warm smile gently creasing the corners of his striking eyes that together fired my passion. I remember how his lips smelled of fruit, how the top of his head was warm to my fingertips. 1923 was to be the year that my life was to become erratic and unpredictable. We married just before my thirtieth birthday, a few months before our child was born.

Jeff suffered badly with lung infections, left over from severe bouts of influenza contracted while on overseas service with the Royal Engineers. The doctors recommended that we move to the coast, where the air would be beneficial to Jeff's condition and in 1932 father bought us a house in Great Yarmouth. Our daughter Dorothy was happy at school, and Jeff had a good job at the local power station.

After a particularly bad bout of coughing, Jeff made an appointment with his doctor who sent him to the hospital for an X-ray. When he returned, he slumped onto the settee, the charismatic smile he had gone out with left behind at the doctor's surgery. Jeff had been diagnosed with tuberculosis at the age of 41. There was nothing the doctors could do, and Jeff died in September of that year.

Without Jeff's wage, life was tough and with a 12 year old to support, my meagre savings soon ran out. We moved back to Bedford and rented a small house close to where my parents were living. Two years later in 1937, mother died. My brothers had their own families to attend to, so it was left to me to look after father at the big house in Rosamond Road.

Dorothy married in 1947, and as there was plenty of room in the house, she and her husband John settled in with me and father. My grandson was born in 1949, and all was well until father started to show some irritation at having a small child in the house. Dorothy and her family moved out, but just a year later father died. He left his three houses to Archie, Bob, and me.

Rosamond Road was far too big just for me, so Dorothy, John and Philip returned and in 1953 my granddaughter was born there. John, though, was clearly not happy and took a new job in Rugby. The house felt empty again, but my niece Sheila Johnson was married in1954 and the couple gladly accepted my invitation to share Rosamond Road until they got on their feet. The arrangement lasted for five years.

At 66 years old, I was finding the train journeys to visit Dorothy were getting tiring, so in 1959 I decided to sell up and start a new life in Rugby. I had just settled into a new routine when after two years, John announced that he was accepting a job offer in Bedford so they were moving back.

I had kept in touch with an old family friend, Reginald Potter, who lived in Denmark Street just a stone's throw from Rosamond Road. Reginald's wife had died ten years before, and we decided to tie the knot. So, I was not far behind Dorothy and her family when they returned to Bedford, and married Reginald in September 1961.

The decade of the sixties passed by very quickly, and by the early seventies Philip and Patricia had left home and married. Dorothy and John's marriage was in disarray, and with my 80th birthday not far away I was feeling my age.

Reginald died in 1975, leaving me alone once again. Dorothy's marriage broke down completely in 1977 and she moved into Denmark Street with me. It felt like we were reliving an old life as mother and daughter.

Olive became very frail and mentally confused. Dorothy arranged for her to be admitted to a nursing home, and for a year she alternated between there and Denmark Street before she died on 4th April 1979 at the age of 85.

Background

Olive's pedigree chart below shows the migration south of her paternal ancestors from Nottinghamshire and those of her maternal line from West Yorkshire to Bedfordshire where Olive was born in 1893. It is impossible to be entirely sure about the accuracy of data from almost half a millennium ago, but more recent generations are included with considerable confidence.

William Johnson
1671-1747
East Retford, Nottinghamshire
|
Joseph Johnson
1688-*1740*
Kenilworth, Warwickshire
|
Robert Johnson
1710-1776
Solihull, Warwickshire
|
Thomas Johnson
1730-*1795*
Easton, Northamptonshire
|
William Johnson
1759-1825
Carlton, Bedfordshire
|
John Reynolds Johnson
1799-1851
Biddenham, Bedfordshire
|
Jesse Johnson
1826-1897
Biddenham, Bedfordshire
|
Robert Johnson
1866-1952
Biddenham, Bedfordshire

George Robinson
1672-*1740*
Wetherby, West Yorkshire
|
John Robinson
1698-*1750*
Patrington, East Yorkshire
|
Henry Robinson
1726-*1778*
Hedon, East Yorkshire
|
Robert Robinson
1750-1812
Wootton, Bedfordshire
|
Samuel Robinson
1777-1858
Wootton, Bedfordshire
|
Samuel Robinson
1808-1896
Houghton Conquest, Bedfordshire
|
James Robinson
1840-1925
Houghton Conquest, Bedfordshire
|
Jemima Jane Robinson
1870-1937
Ampthill, Bedfordshire

Olive Miriam Johnson
1893-1979

Italics = Unconfirmed

Johnson

William Johnson was born in East Retford, Nottinghamshire in 1671, and married Elizabeth Rye from the close-by village of Hayton in 1699. Elizabeth had given birth to an illegitimate son, Joseph, at a young age and William took the child as his own. It was not unusual for adolescent girls to become pregnant in the 1800s, particularly as the age of consent was set at 13 only in 1875. The family moved south to Kenilworth in Warwickshire, and Joseph bore a son Robert with Hannah Nock from Solihull in1710 before being married in Nuneaton in 1711.

Robert Johnson married Elizabeth Robertson from Arlesey, Bedfordshire in 1733 at St. Peter's Church in Pirton, a few miles from Elizabeth's home village. It appears that the couple chose to live about halfway between Solihull and Arlesey as, in 1734, their first child Thomas was born in Easton Maudit, Northamptonshire. Shortly afterwards the family moved to Arlesey where they were to raise Thomas and five more children.

Thomas Johnson's wife Susannah Watts was from Odell, Bedfordshire and they married there in 1759. Their son William was born in Carlton about one mile from Odell. Susan died in 1771 aged 36 giving birth to their second son who they intended to call Thomas after his father, but the child did not survive. Thomas moved to Potterspury in southern Northamptonshire where, in 1799, he drowned himself in the River Great Ouse a short distance along the A5 at Stony Stratford aged 65.

William Johnson married Elizabeth Reynolds from Harrold, not far from Carlton, in 1786 and a few years later the couple moved to Biddenham on the outskirts of Bedford where, on Boxing Day 1799, John Reynolds Johnson was born. Curiously, John was registered using his mother's maiden name as was the next-born Margaret Reynolds Johnson in 1802, although the remaining ten younger and older children were registered simply as Johnsons. John married Elizabeth Cole from Bedford in 1819, and the couple settled down to married life in Biddenham.

On 3rd January 1837, John Johnson was convicted of larceny at Bedford Quarter Sessions and sentenced to transportation for seven years. He sailed on the Neptune from Sheerness on 4th October 1837 for Hobart, Tasmania. Looking back, this seems a harsh sentence for what was probably petty theft, but around 76,000 convicts who committed low level crimes were transported by the British Government between 1804 and 1853. John did not return to England after completing his sentence, and died in Tasmania in 1851.

John's wife Elizabeth remained in Biddenham and brought up their son Jesse, who was 12 years old when his father was deported, and nine other children born between 1820 and 1836. Jesse married Sarah West, also from Biddenham, and their son Robert Johnson, Olive's father, was born in the village in 1866.

Robinson

George Robinson was born in 1672 to Will Robinson from Wetherby, and made a southerly move to the East Riding when he married Elizabeth Chambers from Patrington at St. Patrick's Church in July 1697. The ancient town of Patrington lies about one and a half miles inland, north of the mouth of the River Humber, almost directly opposite Grimsby. The area is presently known as Holderness.

George and Elizabeth's son John was born in the town in 1698. John married Anne Greenshaw, also from Patrington, in December 1726 after their son Henry had arrived in May of that same year. The wedding took place in the neighbouring village of Hedon.

The Robinsons had made Holderness their home for three generations, until Henry Robinson met Sarah Whilney from Yardley Hastings in Northamptonshire. They married at St. Margaret's Church in Sarah's neighbouring village of Denton, during the early summer of 1749. The couple settled in Wootton just across the border with Bedfordshire, where their son Robert was born in 1750.

Robert and his son Samuel Robinson both married local women, so the Robinson family remained in the village. Samuel's wife Elizabeth Handcock bore a son, also Samuel, in 1808 and he wed Lucy Carter from Silsoe in 1831.

Samuel and Lucy settled not far from Silsoe in Houghton Conquest, where their son James was born. James married Emma Gower from Ampthill in 1864, where Jemima Jane Robinson, Olive's mother, and the last of four children, was born.

xvi

Early Years (1893 - 1923)

Olive Miriam Johnson

Olive's parents Robert Johnson and Jemima Jane Robinson married at Biddenham Parish Church on 10th September 1889. Robert was the youngest of eight children, born 18th May 1866 at Ivy Cottage in Biddenham village. His father Jesse was a groom on a local farm, and Robert also worked there as an agricultural labourer from the age of fourteen.

Robert (1866-1952) descended from a long line of farm workers. His father Jesse, grandfather John, great grandfather William from Carlton who married Elizabeth Reynolds in Harrold on 4th April 1786, back through five more generations to his namesake and 7th great grandfather Robert Johnson born in 1651 will all have worked the land. That distant ancestor Robert married Mary Elizabeth Dean from Maryland in the USA who gave him one child, his son William Johnson born 1671. Mary's father William Richard Dean (1627-1699) was born in Dorset, England and was one of the early settlers in Dorchester County in the south east corner of Maryland, USA.

Jemima Jane Robinson (1870-1937) was born in Mount Pleasant, a short cul-de-sac opposite The Rose and Crown in Dunstable Street, Ampthill, although the 1871 census records the family living at 21 Dunstable Street a short time later. Like her husband's ancestors, Jemima's were also farm labourers but from around the Houghton Regis and Wootton areas of Bedfordshire, back until Henry Robinson and her 4th great grandfather John Robinson who were from East Yorkshire. John was baptised on 19th September 1698 at Patrington, a small village in the diocese of York.

At the time of Olive's birth on 23rd November 1893, her father Robert was no longer labouring on farms but worked as a railway carriage examiner on the London and North Western Railway conducting visual checks on their condition. The family lived at 59 Foster Street, and Olive was born at home three years after her brother Archie Edward (1890-1987). Her middle name was taken from her father's sister, Miriam Sarah Johnson. Miriam was born four years after Robert in April 1870, but sadly died at home just nine months later from croup.

Foster Street is in the area of Bedford known as Black Tom, the houses between Tavistock Street and Fosterhill Road. So called because of his swarthy complexion and coal-black hair, Black Tom was a highwayman in the early nineteenth century, an evil character who continued to be feared long after his death. He was hanged and buried with a stake driven through his heart at the junction of Tavistock Street, Union Street and Clapham Road, a spot still known by some as `Black Tom's Grave'. But this did not prevent his ghost haunting the locality in company with another unidentified phantom. In the 1840s, after several apparitions had been seen, people stayed indoors at night for fear of meeting the dreadful pair. The last sighting of Black Tom was around the start of the new millennium when, in broad daylight, a number of witnesses saw a man with a blackened face staggering along Union Street, his head lolling about in the most ghastly fashion, as if he had been hanged. As they watched in fascinated horror the shape faded and vanished into thin air.

Most of the old terraced houses in the area were demolished in the 1960s and replaced with flats, maisonettes and shops.

1 Foster Street, Bedford Then and Now

The birth of Olive's younger brother Robert Victor (1897-1973) meant a move from 59 Foster Street to number 12 to give the family more room. Clapham Road School was not far to walk, and Olive started her education there in 1900. She moved on to Harpur Trust Girls' Elementary School on 30th August 1904 when she turned eleven years of age. The Girls' Elementary was next door to Clapham Road School. In 1901, the family moved again, this time to 15 Battison Street in the centre of Bedford town. Olive's father had left the LNWR in1899, and had become an iron trimmer at W.H. Allen Queens Engineering Works. Older brother Archie moved on from the Harpur Trust Boys' Elementary School on 31st March 1904, also to work at W.H. Allen. Olive left the Girls' Elementary on 25th November 1907 after she turned fourteen.

2 15 Battison Street

    Christmas in 1905 was probably a very merry one, because Olive and her brothers would have learned their mother was expecting a child the following summer. Stanley Johnson was born at their Battison Street home on 2nd September 1906. Tragically, the family's joy was to be short-lived because Stanley caught a thrush infection and died just over two weeks later on 19th September. Jemima was 36 years old, and she would have no more children.

Had Stanley contracted the infection today, he would almost certainly have survived. Treatment with anti-fungal gel produces positive results within a couple of days, and the infection is usually cleared within a week or two. However, even in the present day, if thrush is left untreated it can spread to other organs and result in death.

1907 was to be a turning point in the family's fortunes, because father Robert decided to become a purveyor of beer and spirits. He was granted a licence to sell beer from an ale house at 65 Russell Street (to be redeveloped as Roff Avenue in the 1970s). This whetted his appetite to further his new career, and in December 1908 the family moved to The Burnaby Arms at 66 Stanley Street.

3 The Burnaby Arms

Sadly, neither of the licensed premises produced enough income for Robert to give up his job at the W.H. Allen, so Jemima, son Robert Victor (known as Bob) and Olive helped to run the public house business.

Olive was blessed with a beautiful singing voice, and took lessons after leaving school. The Burnaby Arms gave her an opportunity to practice in front of the local customers, but it wasn't long before she showed her talents to a wider audience. On 8th December 1908, shortly after turning fifteen, Olive sang with a live band at the first ladies' concert of the season in the newly enlarged concert room at the Conservative Club. She was much sought after to perform, but must have wondered if the booking she took for 11th November 1910 to entertain thirty cattle drovers after they had enjoyed a successful tea at St. Mary's Schoolroom in Prebend Street would be well-received. Olive headed the bill for the second part of the programme, and the Bedfordshire Times reported that 'Miss Olive Johnson, though young in years, has an extremely well-trained and sympathetic voice, and gave much pleasure by her two songs, *Down the Vale* and *Violets*.'

Just four years after taking his gigantic leap of faith into the beer and spirits trade, on 31st October 1911 Robert was granted the license for The Gordon Arms at 118 Castle Road, Bedford. Occupying a corner position with Bower Street on one of the main roads leading into the town centre, and central to recently developed housing which had spawned a new community, the public house held much greater potential than the others.

4 The Gordon Arms, Castle Road, Bedford

Olive turned 18 the month after the family moved into The Gordon Arms, younger brother Bob was 13 and still attending school. Archie, at 21, had left home. Olive performed regularly in the pub and responded to calls for her talent across the town and surrounding villages. On 9th October 1913 she returned to her old school at Harpur's Trust where her voice was described as 'full of expression', and sang *All the Girls are Lovely* at the Haynes harvest festival in October 1915.

The Great War of 1914-1918 put much pressure on the pub industry through strict licensing laws imposed by war minister David Lloyd George. His argument was that a sober nation would maximise production of essential items for the war effort. Opening hours were reduced with strict morning and afternoon trading times, early evening closing, a ban on buying drinks for others, and the trebling of beer duty.

Most pubs struggled through the lean times, and luckily Olive was able to provide much needed support to the business from inside the family. Kempston, on the outskirts of Bedford was the garrison for the Bedfordshire Regiment, and the town was a temporary home to many soldiers moving to and from the Western Front. This breathed life into the town's public houses and probably saved many from going out of business.

5 Soldiers from the Argyle and Sutherland Regiment at The Gordon Arms 1914

In August 1914, soldiers from the Argyle and Sutherland Brigade of the Highland Division stationed at Stirling were moved to Bedford, and stayed until December that year when they were mobilised for war and sent to engage in various offensives at the Western Front. The photograph above of them outside The Gordon Arms shows Olive aged twenty and her mother Jemima at a bedroom window, Olive's younger brother Bob standing at the other window, and her father Robert Johnson in a light coloured suit seated to the left of centre in the group.

The photographs below were taken behind The Gordon Arms in 1915, and the top one includes Olive, her parents, her two brothers Bob and Archie, and the family dog in the centre front. That photograph takes the form of a postcard addressed to Olive, and sent from a ship on 24th July 1915.

6 Behind The Gordon Arms 1915

The postcard is written in soft pencil and reads:

> Somewhere on Sea, July 24th 1915
>
> Dear Friend,
>
> Just a line as promised to let you know that my pal and myself are all right. In order to do this I am obliged to send this PC that you gave me because there is nothing else obtainable. We have had a fine voyage. Expect you find things much more quiet there now. Best wishes to all.
>
> D.J. Grove

By the end of the war, both Archie and Bob had joined the Royal Engineers, which left Olive alone to help her parents run The Gordon Arms. Father Robert still had his day job at W.H Allen, so life would have been hectic for the family. It was time for Robert to take stock of his life, and perhaps make the end of the war herald a new beginning. He had turned fifty in 1916 and wanted to spend more time playing bowls and less time working.

In 1922, Archie married Florence Jordan, known to all as Floss. The couple lived just around the corner from The Gordon Arms at 19 Denmark Street. Floss was the fifth of seven children born to Alfred and Emma Jordan of High Street, Henlow. Alfred was an agricultural labourer, and Emma a straw plaiter.

The process of straw plaiting was mainly used in the manufacture of hats and bonnets, and was especially popular in Bedfordshire as a cottage industry for women and children. Most of the women in Henlow High Street are described as a straw plaiter in the 1861 census.

Although selling the plaits to hat manufacturers produced a small additional income, there was a price to pay in terms of oral health. The plaiter would moisten one or two straws at a time with saliva and store them at the sides of her mouth, which often scarred the corner of her lips. She would then draw the straw through her teeth to flatten it, and the sulphur fumes left over from the cleansing process and friction of the straws against the enamel would make her teeth rotten. Often, straw plaiters would have no front teeth left at all.

The industry was often abused by greedy middle-men who insisted the plaiters bought straw from them at an inflated price and then cut payments for trifling imperfections in the finished plaits. It could take about 12 hours to produce 25 yards of plait which, after purchasing the straw and providing a rolling mill and straw splitting tools, might result in payment of around 3d. By the end of the 19th century, cheap imports of straw plait had killed off the cottage industry.

Archie probably met Floss while she was living in as a general servant to the Brown family just around the corner from Foster Street where he was born. James Brown was a commercial traveller working in the chemical industry so probably spent most of his time on the road. The house, at 164 Fosterhill Road in Bedford, is still standing. It comprises four bedrooms and three reception rooms, so his wife, with two daughters and her 62 year old mother to look after, will have needed help around the house.

Although by 1900 much of the open land east of Bower Street had been developed, Pembroke Street, York Street, Denmark Street, Dudley Street and George Street all stopped south of Castle Road. By 1905, most of the houses in these roads continued as far as Goldington Road with only Pembroke Street and York Street stopping at Rosamond Road to the south of Goldington Road School. In 1909, a builder, Henry Jones, purchased land on Rosamond Road to the west of York Street and built five large houses. The first occupier of number 9, Neville Charles Hewitt, a chemist, moved in around 1911.

Robert purchased 9 Rosamond Road, favoured because it was one of only five detached properties in the road, in 1921. The house would stay in the family for almost forty years until 1960, and the author, who lived there from his birth until around the age of five, recalls some of its features with the help of original plans.

The house, although quite large on a generous corner plot, only had four bedrooms. Two were spread between the front and rear to the right of the first floor, while the left side had to fit a central winding staircase, landing and bathroom between smaller bedrooms to the front and rear. The front door opened into a long hallway with stairs to the left, entrances to the front room and sitting room to the right, and dining room and kitchen straight ahead. French doors from the dining room led to a conservatory and toilet at the back of the house.

7 9 Rosamond Road c1925, Robert and Jemima, Morris Bullnose Tourer

The new house was a way for Robert to invest in the future, and the family appear on the electoral register at that address from 1921 onwards even though they still had The Gordon Arms on Castle Road.

Olive would walk back to Rosamond Road each night at closing time after working behind the bar and her regular singing slots. Sometimes, as will become evident later, she did not walk home alone.

8 Olive Johnson c1922

Harry Edwin Jefferies

Harry Edwin Jefferies, who was to become Olive's husband, was born 27th May 1894, about a year after his parents Henry William and Charlotte returned from a military posting in Gibraltar. He was baptised on 4th July 1894 at the Royal Engineer Garrison Church, Brompton. Having a father and grandfather called Henry probably led to naming the child Harry, as that was the spoken form of Henry in medieval England and the names are often interchanged. Harry's middle name Edwin was taken from his father's best friend, army colleague and father-in-law, Edwin Brewer.

The couple lived in married quarters at 14 St. Mary's, Brompton about halfway between Chatham and Gillingham, one of the main Royal Engineer's barracks. It was not permitted for women to give birth within the barracks, so Charlotte was admitted to the Female Hospital at Fort Pitt, part of the garrison at Chatham.

Fort Pitt was originally built around 1805 to protect Chatham's dockyard during the Napoleonic Wars, but was never needed. The main buildings were used for wounded soldiers from the Battle of Waterloo, and by the 1850s became a major military hospital catering for the sick and wounded from the Crimean War and the Indian Mutiny. Florence Nightingale convinced the Liberal government of the time to make Fort Pitt the initial site for the new Army Medical School.

On 29th January, 1900 at the age of six, Harry was admitted to Barnsole Board (Infants) School in Gillingham, following his early attendance at a military school for soldier's children. The family were living at 20 Victoria Terrace. He transferred to the Boys Department on 30th April 1901 a few months before sister Winifred May was born. A year later on 16th April 1902, an entry in the school register notes 'Gone to Northampton' with no further explanation.

The family moved to 13 Hassett Street, Bedford in 1903 following his father's army career change, and on 13th January 1904 Harry was enrolled at the Harpur Trust Boys School at the same time as his younger brother Reginald. A few weeks before his fourteenth birthday, on 8th May 1908, Harry left school to become an apprentice house painter. Little more than a year later, the family's life was turned upside down when his father Henry William Jefferies died in a tragic suicide.

Henry William Jefferies was born in St. Martins Croft in the parish of St. Peter in the southern part of the city of Worcester in January 1861. His father, also Henry, was a gas fitter by trade. Henry Sr. was 26 years old, and his wife Mary Ann 22 when they had their son, the first of five children.

By 1881, when Henry William was 20, his father was manager of the local Gas Works and he was following in his father's footsteps as a gas fitter. Henry's brother Charles was no longer living at home, but he had sisters Margaret (16), Elizabeth (13) and Clara (6) for company. The family lived in Lower Mitton, a chapelry in the parish of Kidderminster. Lower Mitton does not appear on modern day maps, but has been absorbed into the small town of Stourport-on-Severn. Upper Mitton still survives.

Henry joined the Royal Engineers at their main base in Chatham as a sapper on 25th July 1883, taking with him his trade of gas fitter. His army record describes him as 5 feet 8 inches tall with a 42 inch chest, fresh complexion, hazel eyes and brown hair. His first overseas posting was to Bermuda on 30th January 1894 where he remained until being posted to Gibraltar on 9th October 1887.

Although a military presence on Gibraltar was more or less a permanent feature in the late nineteenth century, individual soldiers only spent an average of a couple of years in the garrison before being transferred elsewhere. Henry's posting, however, was to last nearly six years. Only about 10% of soldiers at the garrison were married, and anybody wishing to get married needed special permission to do so. This was rarely granted, unless the soldier was particularly deserving and coming to the end of his term of enlistment. Permission was then sometimes given as an incentive for them to extend their time.

Henry asked for authorisation to marry a few months before his term of enlistment ended, and his request was granted. He married Charlotte Brewer on 22nd February 1893 when he was 32 years old. Charlotte was 21. She was the only daughter of close friend and colleague Edwin William Brewer, a clerk in the Army Service Corps, who was based in Gibraltar at the same time.

Henry and Charlotte returned to Chatham the following June, after which they had six children in fairly quick succession. Harry Edwin (1894), Reginald (1895), Margaret (1897), Claude (1898), Charlotte (1900), and Winifred (1901). By 1901, Henry had been promoted to Quarter Master Sergeant. The couple were living at 20 Victoria Terrace,

Gillingham Road, Gillingham, about a mile from the barracks in Chatham.

Although he had a regular army income, on Christmas Eve in 1902 he spoke to his father-in-law and friend Edwin Brewer and expressed his sorrow that he was unable to afford any presents for his children. Henry threatened to drown himself but Edwin, who was a freemason at the St. Helena Lodge since 1882, loaned him enough money to see him through until he was able to improve his financial position.

In July 1903, the family moved to Bedford where Henry held the position of Sergeant Major Instructor at the Bedford Royal Engineers (Volunteers). Their son Walter was born in 1904, and their eighth and last child Amy Clara in 1906.

Henry retired from the Royal Engineers on 30th April 1908, and the family moved to The Phoenix public house in St. John's Street where Henry had secured the licence. The Phoenix had only opened around the turn of the century, but away from the town centre and at a busy road junction was not in the best of positions to attract a large clientele. After less than a year, Henry gave up the licence and took a job as a collector for the Pearl Life Assurance Society, moving to 38 Aspley Road, a four bedroom terraced house a few hundred yards from St. John's railway station. The house still stands today.

Henry's pension from the Royal Engineers of three shillings and a penny per day, and his wage of twenty five shillings per week as an insurance agent came to about £120 per annum. This was almost double the average salary at the time of about £70 per annum, but not much for such a large family to survive on. Although their eldest child Harry was earning a small wage as a house decorator apprentice, money was still tight and it was not long before tragedy struck the family.

On Saturday 28th August 1909 at around one o'clock on Kimbolton Road, Bedford near the entrance to Hartop's Farm, two young ladies summoned the attention of an errand boy pushing a cart, one Frank Wildman. He found Henry lying on his back with a bottle of spirits of salts next to him (a strong acid used for dissolving cement), and ran to the Kimbolton Road cab rank for assistance. Two of the drivers followed him back to the spot. They lifted Henry onto the cart, and pushed him to the Police Station. From there, two officers took him to the hospital.

Although Henry was treated quickly at the hospital, he was very pale and clearly in great pain. By three o'clock he was dead.

An inquest was held at the hospital the following Monday and the jury found that Henry died from acid poison administered by himself during a fit of temporary insanity.

Henry's funeral was held on Tuesday 31st August 1909. His remains were taken by hearse from the family home at 38 Aspley Road to Foster Hill Road cemetery, where the rector of St. Mary's officiated at the burial service. Henry's coffin was made from polished elm with brass fittings and inscription plate. Present at the service were his wife Charlotte, sons Harry and Reginald, his brother Charles, sister Elizabeth, and father-in-law Edwin Brewer. Also attending were many of Henry's former comrades from the Royal Engineers, who bore the expenses of the funeral.

No longer able to afford the large house in Aspley Road, Charlotte together with her children moved to 36 Dudley Street. Winifred, aged eight and Charlotte, nine, were sent away to be schooled at The Royal Soldiers' Daughters Home, Rosslyn Hill, Hampstead. Reginald, aged 14 was sent to the Royal Engineer Barracks at Brompton, Chatham where his rank in 1911 is described as 'Boy'. Claude, aged ten, was sent to The Duke of York's Royal Military School at Guston, near Dover, to complete his education. Harry, Margaret, Walter and Amy Clara remained with their mother.

Being the eldest of the four children remaining in their new home at 36 Dudley Street, Harry helped out with the family finances with his job as an apprentice house painter and decorator to a firm trading from 49 Commercial Road, Bedford. That was an interesting choice of employment, because Harry was colour blind. This is caused by an inherited faulty gene, and although can be carried by females it generally only affects males. Harry would later pass on the defective gene through his daughter Dorothy to the author, who similarly followed a career path that requires good colour vision - electrical and electronics engineering!

Following in the footsteps of his father and grandfather, Harry decided to join the Royal Engineers and on 14th October 1910 signed up for a period of four years with the 1st Battalion East Anglian Division as a sapper, stationed at Bedford, army number 2201205. He was only sixteen years of age, but a slip of the tongue had his date of birth recorded as 27th May 1893 making him appear one year older than he actually was.

Harry's attestation papers record him as having dark brown hair, brown eyes, being 6 feet tall, weighing 166 pounds and having a 38 inch chest measurement. His physical development was described as good and his vision excellent, although no indication is given that he was colour blind.

After initial training and postings to Thetford, Chepstow, and Great Clacton, Harry was appointed lance corporal. He signed up for a further four years on 10th July 1913, beginning an apprenticeship as an electrician, his aspiration to become a qualified painter and decorator fallen by the wayside.

The war years saw Harry plagued with bouts of influenza, the first of which he contracted in Aden in July 1915. After a long recovery, he returned to Aden only to become sufficiently ill again in September of that year to have to return to England. Harry rejoined his unit on 9th December 1915, but embarked for England on a hospital ship, the H.T. Orsova, shortly afterwards on 18th April 1916 for another three month recovery period.

Harry returned to Egypt, and spent the remainder of WW1 working on the Suez Canal defences, during which time he was promoted to second corporal. He embarked for the last time from Port Said on the H.M.T. Caledonia on 28th May 1919 bound for England.

In 1920, having completed his apprenticeship in the trade of electrician, Harry was re-engaged yet again for a final three year stretch with the Royal Engineers. Between April 1920 and April 1923 he was posted to Tripoli, Palestine and Egypt.

Britain had effectively ruled Egypt since 1882, and when The Great War broke out declared it a British protectorate. The Egyptians were not happy at the way they had been treated during the war, and as soon as the fighting was over they began to push for independence. 1919 saw a series of uprisings, and around 800 Egyptians were killed. In 1922 the British realised that change was unavoidable and declared Egypt an independent sovereign state. The presence of British troops was slowly wound down, but the outbreak of the Second World War in 1939 required the defence of Egypt's borders, and Britain was deeply involved in providing that protection.

Posted to North Africa at the height of the Egyptian Revolution, Harry was promoted to corporal and then sergeant before returning home for demobilisation on 2nd June 1923 after almost thirteen years service.

9 Corporal Harry Edwin Jefferies, Royal Engineers c1920

Harry was awarded four medals for his contribution during WW1. These were (from left to right in the photograph) the 1914-15 Star, the British War Medal, the Victory Medal and the Territorial Efficiency Medal. He also took home with him a thorough training in electrical engineering, evidenced by the apprenticeship he served during his time in the army.

10 Harry Edwin Jefferies WW1 Medals

Unfortunately, medals and a new trade were not the only things Harry took away from his military service. He was also left with badly damaged lungs caused by his frequent severe bouts of influenza. This was to make him susceptible to further infections which would gravely affect the rest of his life.

Building began on the New Electric Light Works in Bedford to provide electricity for lighting homes in 1894, although some houses still relied upon gas lighting in the mid-twentieth century. Foundations were laid in Prebend Street near the approach to the Cauldwell Street bridge by about twenty five men in advance of final tenders being settled. By modern standards, the building was small with a generator room about 60 feet by 30 feet. However, there was a distance of over 100 feet between that room and Commercial Road which would allow an extension to the original plans 'if electric light turns out a success'. The quote here is from the Bedfordshire Times and Independent 2nd June 1894. It is hard to believe that electricity was seen as a technology that might not be taken up.

Initially, there were three engines and generators, with engines supplied by W.H Allen but in 1907 a fourth set was installed which equalled the power output of the original three combined. By then, there would have been no doubt that electric light was to be a success, and as a bonus the hot river water resulting from the steam condensing process was used to heat the new Commercial Road swimming baths.

11 Electric Light Works, Prebend Street, from across the River Ouse

By 1922, the Electric Light Works was an established utility and Harry, with his first class training and excellent conduct reports from his years in the Royal Engineers, had no trouble gaining employment there as an electrician.

The Devonshire Arms public house at 32 Dudley Street was only two doors away from Harry's house at number 36, but less than a quarter of a mile away on Castle Road stood The Gordon Arms. Harry had taken to dropping in there on a Saturday evening to listen to the landlord's daughter. During the week she would mostly be found singing at venues such as Bedford's Corn Exchange, or sometimes in local village halls to support good causes, but she would usually be performing at the Gordon Arms during the weekend. Olive Johnson was very well known in the area.

Although the Gordon Arms run by Olive's father Robert Johnson had plenty of accommodation, the family lived at 9 Rosamund Road which, with a small diversion, happened to lie almost exactly halfway between the public house and Harry's home. One evening, Harry asked if he might walk Olive back to Rosamond Road and their relationship blossomed.

Great Yarmouth (1923-1936)

After that June evening in 1923 when Harry Jefferies asked Olive if he could walk her home, they began to see much more of each other. Later that summer in the grip of a fiery heat-wave, Olive discovered she was expecting a child. She and Harry were quickly engaged to be married, and a wedding hastily set for 27th September.

12 Olive Johnson after her Engagement in 1923 Aged 29

Despite the urgency with which Olive and Harry's wedding was arranged, it turned out to be a grand affair. The ceremony took place at St. Cuthbert's Church, Bedford and was well-attended by family, patrons of The Gordon Arms, fans of Olive's singing and Harry's friends from the Electric Light Works.

Olive was given away by her father, and attended by her two cousins Violet and Daisy Davies, daughters of her paternal aunt Augusta. Harry's best man was his younger brother Claude. Olive's wedding dress was ivory satin trimmed with lace and beads; she wore a veil with a wreath of orange blossoms and carried a bouquet of white carnations. Witnesses at the wedding were Olive's mother and father, and cousin Violet.

A lavish reception was held at East Hall, George Street after which the couple left for a honeymoon in London but not before taking photographs in the garden of 9 Rosamond Road.

13 Olive and Harry with Violet and Daisy (seated) at 9 Rosamond Road

The Bedfordshire Times and Independent carried a full list of the wedding gifts received, which identifies many of the wedding guests. Notable among the names are Mr. and Mrs. Potter and their son Archie Potter, the significance of whom will become clear later.

Following the honeymoon, the couple returned to Bedford where they lived with Olive's parents at Rosamond Road. The house was easily large enough for them all, and having Olive around the home as well as at The Gordon Arms would have been of great benefit to her ageing parents. It was also convenient for Harry, who could keep an eye on his widowed mother just around the corner at 36 Dudley Street.

Dorothy Margaret Jefferies, the author's mother, was born at home on 19th March 1924.

14 Dorothy with Harry, his mother Charlotte, and his Grandparents Edwin and Charlotte Brewer

There do not appear to be any instances of the name Dorothy in either Olive's or Harry's recent ancestry, so they must have gone with the crowd because Dorothy was the second most popular girl's name in 1924, after Mary first and Helen third. Margaret, though, crops up many times amongst Harry's family tree since Margaret Huckle (1814-1894), his great grandmother so he could have suggested that to remember any one of those relatives. Margaret was fifth in the top 200 names of that year, Olive was harshly ranked 198th and Miriam 143rd. The photograph above was taken in the garden at 36 Dudley Street after Dorothy was baptised on 4th May 1924. The ceremony was performed at St. Cuthbert's Church in Bedford, where Olive and Harry were married the previous year. Charlotte Jefferies was Dorothy's godmother.

15 Dorothy c1925

Harry's mother died in the summer of 1926 at the age of 53. Charlotte was still living in the house the family moved to after her husband's suicide in 1909. Her youngest child, Amy Clara would have been twenty, and continued to live at 36 Dudley Street. Tragically, she contracted tuberculosis. In 1935, just after Christmas, she was admitted to Bedford North Wing Hospital and died on 2nd January 1936 at the age of twenty nine. Her death was registered by her brother Walter Jefferies. Amy Clara never married.

Great Yarmouth was a popular seaside resort in the 1920s. It was easily reached by train, had lovely beaches, a magnificent pier and plenty of entertainment. The town was particularly associated with bloaters, a type of cold-smoked herring, which could be posted back home packed in a small wooden box through the Royal Mail. The seaside town became a favourite haunt for Olive and Harry, and they took every opportunity to visit, especially as the sea air was thought to be beneficial to Harry's lungs.

16 Olive and Dorothy Great Yarmouth c 1929

Olive's father Robert retired from The Gordon Arms in January 1929, and her brother Archie took over the license. Although there was plenty of room at 9 Rosamond Road, her father was no longer sharing his time between there and the pub, so Olive and Harry decided to move out to live around the corner at 19 Denmark Street.

Harry was suffering more lung infections as the years went by, caused by their weakening from repeated severe bouts of influenza while he was overseas with the Royal Engineers. He was given medical advice that he should move to an area where the atmosphere was cleaner, and in 1932 the family moved to 83 Palgrave Road in Great Yarmouth to benefit from the cleaner air. Although the house was purchased by Olive's father, the title was held in the name of her mother, Jemima Johnson.

17 83 Palgrave Road, Great Yarmouth

The family was still young and quickly adapted to life at the seaside. Harry was very well qualified after his time in the Royal Engineers and soon found a job as an electrician at the Power Transforming Station, and Dorothy was happy at her new school. They had few money worries because the house was paid for, so Olive could concentrate on providing a relaxed and comfortable home which she hoped would help Harry recover his health.

Great Yarmouth's coal-fired Power Transforming Station was built in 1894, and, with upgrades over the years, by 1923 it generated an output of around 5 Megawatts of power. The coal to generate the steam came both by train and by boat, and water used to cool the condensers was drawn from the River Yare. This was sufficient to provide the basic needs of the region, but even with major generator upgrades as demand for electricity grew it became woefully inadequate. A new power station with an initial capacity of 250 Megawatts came on line in 1959, and the original one was decommissioned in 1961 and demolished soon after.

18 Great Yarmouth Power Transforming Station

Olive's parents visited often for a break by the sea, and during one such visit they dropped off at a local photographer in Great Yarmouth for a set of family photographs.

19 Olive, Mother and Father, and Dorothy Great Yarmouth c1934

The sea air must have helped a little, but Harry continued to suffer lung infections which came to a head in 1935 when he contracted tuberculosis.

Tuberculosis mortality had been reducing over the years leading up to the beginning of The Great War, but it was still very high and produced a significant peak around 1918/1920. By the 1930s, though, it was once again in decline.

Known causes for the spread of tuberculosis included overcrowded living conditions, inadequate ventilation, malnutrition and prolonged physical and mental strain. None of these could account for Harry's ill health. It is thought, though, that by the end of the war nearly all adults were infected to some degree with mycobacterium tuberculosis after exposure to the disease on overseas duty, so it seems likely that the disease could have been lying latent in Harry's lungs for many years and suddenly became active.

Harry was admitted to the General Hospital at Deneside after coughing up serious amounts of blood, and died there with Olive at his bedside on 1st September 1935. He was interred at Caister Old Cemetery, which was used for Great Yarmouth burials from around 1906. The grave location is not known, but is likely to be in Cemetery Section G adjacent to Grave Number 881.

Bedford to Rugby (1936 - 1961)

There was nothing to keep Olive and her daughter in Great Yarmouth after Harry died, and they promptly returned to Bedford. Rather than move back in with her parents, Olive rented 71 Howbury Street. This was within a few minutes walking distance not only from Rosamond Road but also just around the corner from The Gordon Arms, run by her brother Archie. It was also convenient for Goldington Road School, which was important since Dorothy was only twelve years old and not yet eligible to leave full time education.

Yet another tragedy struck in the winter of 1937 when Olive's mother Jemima was taken ill. She was diagnosed with heart disease and died aged 66 on 22nd December.

20 Jemima Jane Johnson c1920

Jemima's funeral took place at Bedford Cemetery, and was very well attended not only by family and friends, but also by customers of The Gordon Arms which she had helped run between 1911 and 1929.

Although her father was not ill, he was into his 70th decade and showing signs of his age. Olive decided to return with her daughter to Rosamond Road to make sure he was well cared for.

The following year on 20th November 1938, a few days before her birthday, Olive attended St. Cuthbert's church in Bedford to see Dorothy confirmed at the age of fourteen. It was only fourteen years earlier that she and Harry had spoken their wedding vows in that same church.

The years through the Second World War were relatively calm for Olive and her father. Archie was busy running The Gordon Arms, and Bob was still at The Phoenix in St. Johns Street where he had been licensee since the late 1920s.

Dorothy joined the Women's Land Army when she reached the eligible age of 19 in 1943, helping to replace the male farm labourers who had been conscripted for the war effort. Much of her time was spent at farms around Sharnbrook, where a massive 18th century town house on the High Street had been turned into a hostel. This provided basic accommodation for scores of Land Girls, with six bunk beds in most of the bedrooms. Apparently they were not allowed to use the grand staircase but had to climb the back stairs, previously used by servants. As Dorothy lived locally, she would have been picked up by truck each day from Rosamond Road rather than stay at the hostel.

In 1944, Dorothy joined the National Fire Service as a dispatcher at the Britannia Road Fire Station. Luckily she was never posted to another location, so was able to continue to help out her mother and grandfather at home. The fire station moved to Barkers Lane, but the old site is still there with its imposing hose tower.

The war years might have been quiet for Olive, but the ones following on were to make up for them. Dorothy was having a serious relationship with one Tony Taylor, who was known as 'Bob' (for his good looks, records the back of a photograph of him). This lasted through 1945 and 1946, but despite Bob having a motor cycle which frequently took the couple to the coast, the relationship came to an end the following year.

Dudley Street flew back into the spotlight when Dorothy spotted John Wadner (the author's father) who lived at number four, just a dozen or so houses further along from where Harry lived when he and Olive met. John had joined the RAF in 1942 and had returned to live with his parents in 1947. His father had signed him up to an apprenticeship as a printer at The Castle Press in 1939 at the age of fifteen, but that was interrupted by the war.

Dorothy and John Wadner were married at St. Cuthbert's Church on 20th September 1947, three days before John's twenty-third birthday. Dorothy was attended by her cousin Molly Keep, two friends Thelma and Margaret Mathers, and two young children Joy Cowper and Geoffrey Eagles. Witnesses to the ceremony were John's mother Violet Wadner and Dorothy's uncle, Walter Jefferies. After the reception at the Dijon for 68 guests, the couple left for a honeymoon in Rye on the East Sussex coast. When they returned they settled into Rosamond Road with Olive and her father.

21 Dorothy and John Wadner wedding

Olive's father was enjoying good health at the age of 82, and still playing bowls almost every day. Twenty six years after first playing in the Bedfordshire County team he applied to be included in one final game for the county. On Saturday 28th August 1948 he played against Warwickshire at Bedford Borough Bowling Club. Still affectionately known to his team-mates as 'Bobbie', he had assisted at Bedford Bowling Club for over twenty years and at one time was President of Russell Park Bowling Club.

John completed his apprenticeship in October 1948, and the couple were expecting a child the following Spring. Even though there was plenty of room at Rosamond Road, with her aged father living there Olive decided to pay for Dorothy to give birth in the Rena Nursing Home at 26 DeParys Avenue. The cost of one week in the nursing home, including Dettol at 4s.6d. and laundry at 17s.6d, was £9.13s.6d. Nearly £10 at the time is equivalent to around £355 in 2020. The receipt for a second week, which includes Ostermilk but no Dettol, adds £11.8s.9d making just over £21 in total, or about £750 today. Nursing home births are rare now, with most being performed at home or in hospital, but if available would likely cost far in excess of £750 for two weeks care.

Olive's grandson, Philip, was born in the early hours of Saturday 9th April 1949. Dorothy and John had little by way of savings, and it was only recently that John had completed his apprenticeship and was earning a better wage. Olive made sure the couple, and especially her new grandson, didn't want for anything. Walks around the park in a new pram, trips to the seaside, visits into town, nothing was too much. Philip even enjoyed a head start with reading, attending early lessons with a tutor, Mrs. Lennox, directly across Rosamond Road at number 12.

Olive's father Robert was into his eighties when Philip was born. Much as Olive wanted her daughter and family to live with her, they were becoming more of an irritation to her father, who was showing signs of dementure. In 1951 Dorothy, John and Philip moved out of Rosamond Road half a mile away to an upstairs flat at 62 Goldington Avenue.

Just over a year after Dorothy moved out, Robert took a turn for the worse and was admitted to Springfield House, Kempston, a private asylum built in 1837 with the objective to relieve overcrowding at the County Asylum in Ampthill Road. However, 'pauper lunatics' were left behind and only private patients were transferred across. By the 1950s the facilities had expanded to incorporate up-market activities such as billiards, tennis and boating and advertised vacancies 'for both Ladies and Gentlemen'.

Robert was also suffering from advanced prostate problems and he died from uralmia (retention of urine) and chronic prostatitis at Springfield House on 3rd August 1952 aged 86. Even though he had spent decades as a well-known Bedford publican, and was a much-admired bowls player for the town and county, there is no mention of his death nor funeral in the local newspapers. It is possible that in his final years he shied away from his old friends and acquaintances, or perhaps Olive and her brothers simply did not want any fuss. Regrettably, that means there is no public record of where Robert is buried.

22 Robert Johnson c1920

Robert's will, drawn up in 1939, left £50 to his son Archie, £25 to the Bedford County Hospital, £25 to Welfare of the Blind, and all of his furniture and household items to Olive. The rest of his estate was to be divided one third to Archie and one third to Bob, but with the remaining third held in trust to pay Olive an income during her lifetime. A codicil added in 1945 distributed specific properties: 182 Castle Road to Archie, 9 Rosamond Road to Olive, and 62 George Street to Bob. Probate was granted to Archie on 20th September 1952, with effects valued at £9221 6s 8d.

Rather than leave Olive alone with her thoughts and an empty house, Dorothy and her family moved back to Rosamond Road. It was there, less than a year later on 14th April 1953, that Olive's second grandchild Patricia Margaret was born. The author vaguely remembers being allowed to visit his sister in the bedroom where she was born, and offering her a custard cream biscuit. He ate it himself shortly afterwards.

John was six years out of his apprenticeship and doing well at The Castle Press as a printing machine minder. However, with two children to support, he decided to throw out some feelers for an improved position. In the autumn of 1954 he applied for a management job at a new printing company in Rugby, Albert Frost & Sons.

Frosts offered a commencing salary of £12 per week, £624 per annum (equivalent to about £330 per week, £17160 pa in 2020). This is only half the present day average salary for someone in full time work, but higher than the average in 1954 of £9 per week. The company also bought a three bedroom house at 2 Anderson Avenue in a pleasant area of Rugby close to schools and shops, which the family would enjoy free of rent and rates for the duration of John's employment. By Christmas, they had left Bedford for a new life.

After her daughter and her young family had gone to Rugby, Olive was left alone at Rosamond Road. With its large sitting room, lounge, and dining room downstairs and four bedrooms upstairs, the house was far too big for one person. Olive was 61, the house took a great deal of looking after and, although she had no rent or mortgage to pay, the upkeep was expensive.

23 2 Anderson Avenue, Rugby c1955

Olive's brother Archie was fast approaching retirement and no longer running The Gordon Arms. 1953 was Elizabeth II's coronation year, and the story goes that Archie gave the author a Coronation Crown with a promise that he would have another when he reached the age of 21. Bob had been the licensee at The Phoenix public house in St. John's street since before the Second World War and was still there. Seven years junior to his brother, he was starting to think about hanging up his glass cloths. Although they enjoyed a good relationship, and Olive spoke fondly of her brothers Archie and Bob and their wives, they rarely visited Rosamond Road.

Relief arrived in the form of Olive's niece Sheila, the third and last child of brother Bob. Sheila married Howard Wilmott, a builder's labourer, in January 1954 and had nowhere to live. Olive, on the other hand, was rattling around using only one of four large bedrooms at Rosamond Road. Sheila and Howard moved in with Olive to their mutual benefit.

Living forty miles apart does not sound far these days, but travel was not so easy in the fifties. Luckily in the decade before Beecham's plans for major restructuring of the railways which would drastically reduce the network, there was an excellent service between Bedford and Rugby.

The trains, though, were far less comfortable than now. Some carriages had a corridor linking compartments, but mostly once you had boarded you were stuck with the compartment you entered from the platform, including any incumbent passengers.

John's older brother Peter Wadner had passed on his Hillman Minx car before Dorothy's family left for Rugby. The car was in excellent order, and all that was required was the replacement of two tyres, purchased for £8.14s at Lichfield's Garage in York Street. As well as repeated trips between Rugby and Bedford, the old car made some quite adventurous journeys over the years and the author has no recollection of it ever breaking down. The longest was probably Rugby to Llandudno in North Wales for a holiday in the mid-fifties.

24 Hillman Minx 10HP

Between the railway system and being fetched by car, Olive was able to make frequent visits to Rugby, and often joined in holidays. On more than one occasion the family spent a week in a caravan on top of the cliffs at East Runton in North Norfolk.

25 East Runton c1955 Olive with Dorothy, Philip and Patricia

Life for Olive at Rosamond Road in the late fifties held few events of note, although not so for one of her brothers.

Bob's wife of forty years, Edith, died on 9th December 1958 aged 62. Nine months later, on 26th September 1959, Bob remarried to Dorothy Bishop, known to all as Dot. Bob and Dot continued to live in his house at 62 George Street, just a stone's throw from Olive.

Archie was living at the house left to him by his father at 182 Castle Road with Floss, so was not far from Olive either. Around 1957, Archie sold it and moved to 33 King Edward Road, off Barkers Lane in the Goldington area of Bedford.

Even though Olive was in good health, the trips to Rugby were becoming wearing and happened less frequently as the years passed. What began as a stop-gap sharing her home with Sheila and Howard continued for five years. Although beneficial to both parties, the arrangement came to a conclusion when, in 1959 at the age of 66, Olive made a bold decision to move to Rugby to be close to her daughter and grandchildren.

The cost of removing her belongings forty miles from Bedford to Rugby on 28th April 1959 was £12 plus insurance in transit of 7s, which covered £200's worth of items. Because Olive's new house at 1 William Street was quite small, there was not very much she could take with her and most of the furniture at Rosamond Road was sold.

26 Number 1 William Street, Rugby, Present Day

William Street is located in an older area of Rugby off Railway Terrace, which leads to the railway station past what many years ago was the town's cattle market, now marked only by the appropriately named Drover Close. Close by is Lawrence Sheriff School, which originally provided extra places for boys from Rugby School as the town expanded in the eighteenth century. By 1878 there was an ever-growing need for places at the school, and a new Lower School was built on the present site at what was then the eastern limit of the town's built-up area. It was this Lower School that would become a grammar school for boys, Lawrence Sheriff School as it is presently known.

The houses in William Street are mostly 'two up two down', and number 1 is no exception. Two fairly large bedrooms and a bathroom upstairs, and a front room, dining room and small kitchen downstairs. Like many older buildings there was a cellar, reached via a door in the dining room, with stone steps leading down to a grimly lit area with the same footprint as the house. Towards the front of the cellar a small window about four feet wide and two feet high opened to allow access to the area beneath an iron grid in the pavement.

Although William Street is the opposite side of the town to Anderson Avenue, a frequent bus service made it easy for Olive to make the journey of about a mile and a half.

27 Olive visiting 2 Anderson Avenue, Rugby c1959

When Olive moved to Rugby, Patricia was in the second year at Rokeby Primary School, about two hundred yards along Anderson Avenue. Philip, four years older, was about to start his final year at the school. Olive was in the audience when he played the postman in Pinocchio at the school pantomime, and also mid-year when he sat alone cross-legged centre stage playing snake charming music on a recorder, with a snake (old bicycle inner tube) being pulled out of a wicker basket on a length of thin thread by a helpful teacher stage right.

Almost twenty five years after Harry had died, and with renewed vitality and purpose in life through being close to her daughter and grandchildren, Olive began a platonic relationship with a new man.

28 Olive and Walter (and Patricia behind bench) Caldecott Park c1959

Known to the family as Walter or, for reason unknown, 'Pop' he became an important part of Olive's life. Sadly, Walter died on 19th May 1960.

That same year, Olive was delighted to discover that her grandson had passed his 11+ and would be attending Lawrence Sheriff School from September. The school was only a few minute's walk from William Street and Philip turned up for lunch a few times each week. Fortunately for the author, Olive was not a creative cook so the food was never haute cuisine. She did, however, serve up delicious pies with thick onion gravy. The school refectory was adequate, but it is difficult to beat a home-made meat pie.

Full Circle - Back to Bedford (1961-1979)

Reginald Potter had attended Olive's wedding to Harry in 1923, with his wife Rose and one-year-old son Archie. Archie was named after Rose's brother. Reginald and Rose (nee Richardson) had married in the summer of 1921, and lived in Rose's family home at 40 Garfield Street, just around the corner from The Burnaby Arms which Olive's father had kept before The Great War. The Johnsons and Richardsons knew each other sufficiently well for Reginald, Rose and Archie to be invited to Olive's wedding.

Rose died in 1934 when Archie was just twelve years old, and Reginald married Maud Bloomfield, a milliner from Ipswich, in 1935. Maud had first been married in 1917, but her husband was killed in France in 1918. The couple moved to 12 Denmark Street, although Reginald did not sell Garfield Street but rented it out instead.

Reginald's son Archie was a lance corporal in the Royal Engineers during the Second World War. At the age of 22 he was killed in action by a land mine in Italy on 27th July 1944, and buried at the Ancona War Cemetery. Seven years later, in 1951, Maud died leaving Reginald without his wife and son. Hanging from the porch at 12 Denmark Street was a new sign: Archie's Cottage.

Olive had kept in touch with Reginald while living at Rosamond Road, a stone's throw from Denmark Street, and continued to exchange occasional letters after she moved to Rugby.

John was offered a job at E.J. Day, a printing company in Bedford in the spring of 1961. It would be a major upheaval, taking Philip out of Lawrence Sheriff after only one year at the school, Patricia had made many friends in Rugby and didn't want to leave them behind, and Olive had only moved to be close to them a couple of years before. The job, though, gave John control over the whole printing process as Works Manager and brought with it a significant increase in salary. It would mean the family would be in a much better financial position, he could afford to buy a house, and as a bonus would be back in familiar territory with his parents, brothers and sisters.

Olive was never going to stay in Rugby with her family back in Bedford. Coincidentally she had recently heard from Reginald, who was clearly unhappy living by himself. They arrived at a simple solution which would give Reginald the companionship he had missed since Maud died ten years earlier, and give Olive a secure home, once again close to her family.

Olive and Reginald married locally at Christ Church on 2nd September 1961 and settled in to a quiet life together at Archie's Cottage.

29 Olive and Reginald Potter c1962

John accepted the job at E.J. Day, and the family returned to Bedford in the summer of 1961. A huge project had started in 1953 to build houses on open farmland to satisfy increased demand for homes from the people of Bedford. By 1958 some two thousand houses had been built, including two parades of shops and two public houses. John purchased one of the houses constructed for private sale, a three bedroom property at 32 Furzefield close to the Queens Drive shops and the Queens Tavern public house.

Although Patricia managed to get a place at a local primary school, there were none available at the Bedford grammar so after the end of the summer holidays Philip had to bus to Stratton School at Biggleswade each day, a twelve mile journey by coach each way.

Tuesdays were always special at Furzefield, because that was Olive's regular day to visit. She never failed to turn up with a bar of Frys Chocolate Cream for Patricia and Turkish Delight for Philip. This chocolate bar ritual continued every week until at least 1965 when Philip left home at the age of sixteen. Patricia probably enjoyed double helpings from then onwards.

One of Olive's favourite haunts was The Devonshire Arms in Dudley Street.

30 The Devonshire Arms, Dudley Street, Bedford

Reginald was not keen on alcohol, but it flowed in Olive's blood after growing up in one public house after another. Almost unnoticeable unless you walk past it, the 'Devon' is tucked between numbers 30 and

34 halfway along the southern end of the street and just two houses away from where Harry lived before he and Olive met and were married.

The alley alongside the pub leads through to Denmark Street, a few houses from Archie's Cottage, and every evening after tea Olive would make her way to the door at the right next to the cellar access. The door opened into the 'snug', which had just one small table and two rather uncomfortable-looking wooden dining room chairs. Through a hatch in the wall she would order a bottled Guinness. While sipping her drink, Olive smoked the one Olivier filtered cigarette she allowed herself each day, and after half an hour would return home.

Life was fairly settled for Olive and Reginald in Denmark Street. In 1962 Archie and Floss moved from Goldington to a newly built bungalow at 73 Heronscroft not far from Dorothy's house in Furzefield. Bob died in1973, and Dot moved to 55 Denmark Street not far from Archie's Cottage.

During the decade between the mid sixties and mid seventies, Olive saw much change in Dorothy's life. Philip was living away from home, although he returned some weekends and occasionally for a stretch of a few months depending on where his apprenticeship attachments took him. In 1968 he was permanently based at ICL's research and development laboratories in Stevenage, and having graduated from two wheels to four he was able to travel from Bedford each day.

Philip had clearly inherited one particular gene from Olive, because he took a job as barman at The Queen's Tavern just around the corner from Furzefield, working three nights and Saturdays and Sundays each week. It was there in 1969 just before the first moon landing that he set eyes on Christine Brooker across the off license counter. Seven months later, in February 1970, Philip and Christine were married. One year after their wedding they moved to Stevenage.

31 Philip, Olive and Patricia at Furzefield c1968

John was doing very well at E.J. Day, and spotted a rare opportunity to climb the property ladder. Between 1968 and 1971, the government was looking at sites for a third London airport. The commission published its recommendations in 1971, but the results were rejected and three of the four options remained on the table. One of the short-listed candidates was RAF Thurleigh, close to Bedford, built in 1940 for Bomber Command. This news caused a massive fall in property prices in the surrounding villages, and John bought a beautiful house in Carlton, a pretty village a few miles outside Bedford, for a song.

By 1973, RAF Thurleigh was taken off the table as a candidate for the airport and John cashed in by selling the property in Carlton and moving back to Bedford to a smaller three bedroom property in Heronscroft, a few dozen houses from where Olive's brother Archie and Floss lived. Patricia married Keith Ashpole in the autumn of 1975, and with both children having flown the nest, tensions which had built up over many years between Dorothy and John bubbled to the surface.

Once again Olive's life took a tragic turn when her husband Reginald died in July 1975. He bequeathed Olive a small amount of cash in his will, but more importantly he left Archie's Cottage in trust with his nephews for her to live in as long as she wished. Within a matter of weeks, Olive also lost her sister-in-law Floss.

John gave up his career in the printing business in 1977 and became caretaker for Rutherford School in Bedford. There was a house attached to the caretaker's job, so Heronscroft was sold to move into the free accommodation.

Olive by now was 84 years old and, nearly three years after Reginald died, was becoming quite frail. Living alone, she was a constant worry to Dorothy and this only served to increase the stress between her and John, who insisted upon a separation. Dorothy left the matrimonial home and moved into Archie's Cottage with Olive. John petitioned for divorce, and in July 1978 the marriage of over thirty years was declared by the courts to be over.

By the beginning of 1978 Olive had become mentally confused. Dorothy was finding the situation difficult to cope with, and Olive was admitted to the Cheltondale Nursing Home at 82-84 Castle Road. For more than a year she alternated between nursing homes and Archie's Cottage.

On 9th January 1979, Olive was moved to Lansglade House Care Home in Lansdowne Road, Bedford. She died there after suffering a stroke on 4th April 1979, less than half a mile from where she had been born 85 years earlier.

Olive was cremated and her ashes scattered in the Garden of Remembrance at Bedford Cemetery in Fosterhill Road.

Epilogue

Under the terms of Reginald's will, there was no provision for Dorothy to continue living at Archie's Cottage after Olive's death and the house was sold. Dorothy rented a small bed-sit not far from the school where John had briefly been caretaker and made a new life for herself. In 1983 at the age of 59 she died from bowel cancer.

Archie continued living in Heronscroft for twelve years after losing Floss, and achieved the grand age of 97 before passing in 1987. Philip never collected the second Coronation Crown.

Patricia was only 47 when she discovered that a bout of summer influenza turned out to be pancreatic cancer. Within three months of the diagnosis she died at home on 26th October 2000.

Shortly after her husband Jeff's death in 1935, Olive purchased for one guinea a Grant of Exclusive Right of Burial in Cemetery Section G, Grave Number 881. There is little doubt that she wished to be laid to rest next to him when the time came. Regrettably Olive's wish was not carried out, even though she died within the 50 year time span of the grant.

    Harry will have a long wait.

www.ingramcontent.com/pod-product-compliance
Lightning Source LLC
Chambersburg PA
CBHW072014060426
42446CB00043B/2548